*Enter into the
anticipation of the ages for
the marvels of God's unfolding
plan. Let this story leap off the
pages of Scripture and into your
heart again. Savor the moment
when God became
one of us.*

the Wonder of Advent

DEVOTIONAL

*Experiencing
the Love and Glory of the
Christmas Season*

CHRIS TIEGREEN

TYNDALE
MOMENTUM™

*The nonfiction imprint of
Tyndale House Publishers, Inc.*

Visit Tyndale online at www.tyndale.com.

Visit Tyndale Momentum online at www.tyndalemomentum.com.

TYNDALE, *Tyndale Momentum*, and Tyndale's quill logo are registered trademarks of Tyndale House Publishers, Inc. The Tyndale Momentum logo is a trademark of Tyndale House Publishers, Inc. Tyndale Momentum is the nonfiction imprint of Tyndale House Publishers, Inc., Carol Stream, Illinois.

The Wonder of Advent Devotional: Experiencing the Love and Glory of the Christmas Season

Copyright © 2017 by Chris Tiegreen. All rights reserved.

Cover illustration by Eva Winters. Copyright © Tyndale House Publishers, Inc. All rights reserved.

Designed by Ron Kaufmann

Published in association with the literary agency of Mark Sweeney and Associates, Naples, FL 34113

Scripture quotations are taken from the *Holy Bible*, New Living Translation, copyright © 1996, 2004, 2015 by Tyndale House Foundation. (Some quotations may be from the 2004 edition of the NLT.) Used by permission of Tyndale House Publishers, Inc., Carol Stream, Illinois 60188. All rights reserved.

ISBN 978-1-4964-1909-5

Printed in China

23   22   21   20   19   18   17
7   6   5   4   3   2   1

For Timothy

INTRODUCTION

IN A SMALL TOWN in Judea long ago, God clothed himself in flesh and began to live among us. It was a stunning move, revolutionary in its purpose, and it is still changing lives today. There's a reason the first coming of Jesus is so celebrated, and we don't want to miss it. By God's invitation, this is a story we can enter into every day.

That's the purpose of this devotional—to go deeper into the account of Christ's birth and to focus our thoughts on the riches of its meaning. We want not only to appreciate what happened in Bethlehem more than two millennia ago; we want to experience it in our lives right now.

Advent is a time of anticipation and joy, but it can also be a time of busyness and stress. The turmoil of the season can distract us from the true message—though it may also lead us to long for a Savior. Either way, in the depths of our hearts, we have not forgotten what the celebration is all about. We know it's a story that changed the world forever. And we desire to embrace it fully.

The readings in this book all point toward that goal. After a week of short daily readings leading into the Advent period, each devotion draws from a biblical text, explores its original context and its meaning for us today, prompts a time of reflection and prayer, and includes a quote from the wealth of Christmas music that has been passed down to us across eras and cultures. Taken together, these elements enable us to savor this remarkable divine story each day.

Throughout these readings, we will recall the prophecies of the coming Messiah and our desperate need for him, celebrate the announcement that he would come through a young woman named Mary, and meditate on the pregnancy of God's promises and our hope in them. We will take a few minutes each day to let the significance of the Nativity sink in and explore what it means for our lives and our world. This season is a special time on the calendar, but it's so much more. It is not only a time to remember a long-ago event; it's a time to experience God himself.

Preparation

24

PHILIPPIANS 2:6-11

He gave up his divine privileges;

he took the humble position of a slave

and was born as a human being.

PHILIPPIANS 2:7

ADVENT celebrates the Incarnation—the divine taking on human flesh. One of the briefest but most profound summaries of this story is a poetic excerpt in Philippians 2, which describes how the Son left the privileges of deity behind when he came from heaven to earth. He entered human flesh to be like us, but also to be something more—humanity as we were designed to be, unfallen and filled with the presence of God. He showed us what a human being can do by faith when fully submitted to the Father. Prepare your heart this week by reflecting on Christ's purpose in coming to this world as an infant.

REFLECTION

How does God becoming flesh redeem the human race? What do you think the Incarnation was like for Jesus?

25

JOHN 6:35-40

I have come down from heaven to do the will of God

who sent me, not to do my own will.

JOHN 6:38

WHY DID JESUS COME TO EARTH? He gives several purpose statements in the Gospels, and we will explore some of them this week in preparation for Advent. In John 6, Jesus said he came to do the will of the Father— and that the will of the Father was to call people to faith and to raise them up at the last day. In other words, this was a divine rescue mission. The ministry of Jesus consistently demonstrated his desire to save. Even his birth stories reflect God's purpose—in reaching shepherds, magi from the East, people longing to see the Messiah—and give us clues as to the nature of his mission.

REFLECTION

What did Jesus come to save you from? What did he come to save you for?

26

MARK 1:35-39

Jesus replied, "We must go on to other towns as well,
and I will preach to them, too. That is why I came."

MARK 1:38

JESUS DID NOT remain in one place. It's true that he never
ventured far beyond Judea and Galilee, but he had some
influence among Gentiles and sent his followers into all
nations before he ascended. What began in a village called
Bethlehem was intended to reach into every corner of the
world—a single seed that would cover the planet with its
growth. This is why he came. The Incarnation—the life,
ministry, death, and resurrection of Jesus—was the central
event in a global mission.

REFLECTION

What does it say about God's mission that the Nativity took place in Bethlehem rather than in a more prominent place?

MATTHEW 10:34-36

Don't imagine that I came to bring peace to the earth!

I came not to bring peace, but a sword.

MATTHEW 10:34

THE NIGHT OF JESUS' BIRTH, the angels declared "peace on earth" to the shepherds in the fields (Luke 2:14). But Jesus said peace was not his mission. Why the discrepancy? Because God does want peace—the *shalom* of his Kingdom—to invade the hearts and lives of those who seek him. But it's also clear that the message of Jesus would be controversial to many, exposing hearts and dividing loyalties. Humanity will never be fully united in faith before God makes all things visible at the end of the age. Yes, he wants us to be at peace—*in him*. But many will not accept peace on those terms. The Messiah's mission was—and still is—contested.

REFLECTION

In what ways do you see opposition to Jesus' mission today? How does it play out in your life?

28

Don't misunderstand why I have come. I did not come
to abolish the law of Moses or the writings of the prophets.
No, I came to accomplish their purpose.

MATTHEW 5:17

A LITERAL TRANSLATION of Romans 10:4 says Christ is
the "end of the law." But does that refer to the aboli-
tion of God's law or the fulfillment of it? If the latter, which
seems to be the clear meaning in light of Jesus' words, then
our salvation implies change. Jesus not only lived up to the
law's requirements; he also puts a righteous nature within
us. He did not come to tell us to be good; he came to make
us new. The law gave us a standard but no power to meet
it. Jesus came to transform us from within.

REFLECTION

Why is it necessary for us to be made new? How does the Incarnation—the divine nature in the flesh—foreshadow what God wants to do in us?

29

The Spirit of the Sovereign LORD is upon me, for the

LORD has anointed me to bring good news to the poor.

He has sent me to comfort the brokenhearted

and to proclaim that captives will be released

and prisoners will be freed.

ISAIAH 61:1

JESUS QUOTED this messianic prophecy from Isaiah when he taught at his hometown synagogue in Nazareth and declared the prophecy to be fulfilled (Luke 4:16-21). If we want to know what God-in-the-flesh is like and what he intends to accomplish in our lives, this is it: He brings good news, meets the needs of the poor, comforts the broken-hearted, and releases captives, reaching into every area of fallenness—spiritual, physical, emotional, relational . . . all of it. The child in Bethlehem came with a comprehensive mission to bring God's Kingdom into our lives.

REFLECTION

What do you need God to accomplish in your life? What aspect of Jesus' ministry applies most to your situation today? How does his promise stir up your faith to receive this renewal?

He has sent me to tell those who mourn

that the time of the LORD's favor has come.

ISAIAH 61:2

I SAIAH'S MESSIANIC PROPHECY—one among many—
promises a crown of beauty in the place of ashes, a blessing in the place of mourning, and dancing and praise in
the place of despair. As people who have experienced the
wounds and brokenness of living in a fallen world, that's
really good news for us to hear. We long for beauty, blessing, and dancing. We need this coming Messiah. And we
need him to be very real in our lives.

REFLECTION

In what places of ashes and mourning would you like God to provide restoration? What holes in your heart do you want him to fill?

Advent prayer

Lord, may Jesus be more real to me this season than he ever has been. Open my eyes wider than ever to the beauty of his coming. Give me ears to hear the whispers of your voice. May your restoration continue and your Kingdom come—in my life, in my family, in my workplace, in my church, in my community, in my world—just as it is in heaven. May I live with excited anticipation throughout this season and beyond. Grant that I would enter into the story and the blessing of the Christ child more fully each day. Amen.

1

Out of Darkness

ISAIAH 9:1-7

The people who walk in darkness will see a
great light. For those who live in a land of
deep darkness, a light will shine.

ISAIAH 9:2

ONE NIGHT long ago, angels broke into the darkness
to sing about the birth of a very special child. Their
audience was not assembled in a public square or a king's
court. The angels spoke to shepherds sitting in the gloom,
protecting their sheep from predators and preventing any
from wandering. It was a scene rich with meaning—among
his many wonderful attributes, God is a master of poetic

imagery—as these menial workers witnessed history's most stunning news. Not only was their darkness pierced by the brilliance of heaven, but so was the earth's.

Scripture says the world walks in darkness, and we can hardly dispute the fact. For all our claims of enlightenment, we continue to build ourselves up and tear one another down. We have made amazing technological advancements but remain bound by short life spans and finite understanding. Egos, greed, bitterness, deception, and wars have not gone away. Many people have not only given up their search for truth; they have begun to deny it even exists. As a whole, we have embraced the darkness as normal.

There's a world of difference between what's usual and what's normal; between our experiences of the way things are and our hopes for the way they should be. Our eyes may be adjusted to the darkness of the world, but they were made for brighter vision. We have been designed to see and experience glory. We are destined for a brighter realm. We are called to come into the light.

That's what Advent is all about. The coming of Christ,

the incarnation of God himself, is an invasion of light into a dark world. It is the Creator's plan to establish a new normal for anyone willing to embrace it by faith. The ancient prophecies assure us that a light will shine in the land of deep darkness and that the people whose eyes are dimmed by hopelessness will see something much, much better. Those promises began to be fulfilled with the coming of the Christ, the Savior, the Messiah from a realm of glory. The darkness has been pierced—by brilliant angels for one night and by the child of promise for the ages. The dawn is coming for anyone willing to see it with new eyes.

Prayer

Lord, open my eyes. Awaken my hope. Show me your realms of glory that I may walk in the light of truth and eternity, now and forever. Amen.

REFLECTION

Where do you see darkness in this world? Where do you see light? Which one most captures your attention?

Further reading: John 8:12

A thrill of hope, the weary world rejoices,

for yonder breaks a new and glorious morn.
"O HOLY NIGHT" ("CANTIQUE DE NOËL"),
PLACIDE CAPPEAU

2

No Longer Captive

ISAIAH 9:1-7

You will break the yoke of their slavery

and lift the heavy burden from their shoulders.

You will break the oppressor's rod.

ISAIAH 9:4

Perhaps the words *yoke* and *slavery* seem a little harsh. After all, freedom has become one of the highest values of civilization. Americans sing about the land of the free and the home of the brave, not the plight of captives and the yoke of the slave. People around the world are proud of their independence and join in the fight for human rights and freedoms. We are no longer captive to anyone.

Or are we? As much as we try to live selfless lives, our focus is relentlessly drawn back to ourselves. As much as we've tried to overcome bad habits, destructive thought patterns, broken relationships, sinful tendencies, and guilt and shame, we often remain gripped by their unyielding influence. And as much as we have fought against the specter of death, everyone eventually succumbs to it. So we think we are free, yet we serve ourselves; we think we are independent, but we need help; and we think we are invincible—until we have to give in to greater forces. And we inevitably do. If we're not careful, even our freedom to choose will make us captive to our own desires. Humanity's attempts at independence from God have enslaved us to much worse masters. We were not made for self-sufficiency.

How can we escape that cycle? Certainly not by breaking it on our own. No, we need an intervention from beyond, a completely new way of living, another genesis that gives us a fresh start with a different mind and heart. The good news of the Incarnation is that God has recreated humanity in his own image, even better than at first.

He has given us not only an example of a truly free life; he has empowered us to live in that freedom. The child born in Bethlehem broke all bonds, defied all norms and expectations, and even conquered death, and his Spirit is implanted in those who believe. That means we can break bonds, defy norms and expectations, and overcome death too. Life doesn't get any freer than that.

Don't waste the extraordinary gift of the Incarnation by continuing to live in captivity—to habits, patterns, shame, self, others' expectations, *anything*. In Christ, wounds can be healed, sin can be broken, and death is overcome. Jesus was born into this world in order to set us free.

Prayer

Father, forgive me for any attempts at independence from you, whether intentional or not. Liberate me from the power of sin and the wounds it has created. I flee from every false master and gladly accept the freedom of your grace. Amen.

REFLECTION

Is anything holding you back from living as a completely new, absolutely accepted, fully empowered child of God? If so, what would it take to leave those shackles behind and walk in freedom?

Further reading: John 8:34-36

He is the Messiah indeed,
King of the universe,
who gives us back life by
breaking our chains.

"OH! WHAT A GREAT MYSTERY" ("AH! QUEL GRAND MYSTÈRE"), FRENCH CAROL

3

Child of Mystery

ISAIAH 9:1-7

For a child is born to us, a son is given to us.

The government will rest on his shoulders. And

he will be called: Wonderful Counselor, Mighty

God, Everlasting Father, Prince of Peace.

ISAIAH 9:6

I T MUST HAVE SOUNDED ABSURD. Over the centuries, we've grown accustomed to the words quoted from pulpits, sung to us in an oratorio, and printed on Christmas cards. But really, a child who would be called Everlasting Father? A human who would be called Mighty God? Could the prophet really expect anyone to receive the counsel of a boy or entrust the government to him?

These short sentences were a prophetic enigma, surely intentionally cryptic, and mind-bending for anyone who had never heard them before. They were hidden in mystery.

But now the plan has unfolded. Looking ahead from the point of Isaiah's prophecy centuries before Jesus was born, the sages must have been puzzled. Looking back, we can see exactly what Isaiah meant. The child was human, to be sure, but he was more, born of divine and human parentage. He stepped into this realm from eternity and would step back out of this realm and into eternity again. These paradoxes—and many more in his Kingdom—were absolutely true. This child, above all others, could give wonderful counsel and comfort. This human, distinct from all others, would come to be known as the mighty God and everlasting Father. This royal prince would have a Kingdom like no other, won from conflict but bent on peace. He was—and is—an intersection of earthly and heavenly realms, a doorway between our visible world and eternal realities, the child who would be Lord.

Even looking back on history, we have a hard time

understanding exactly what happened in the Incarnation. But God is much more interested in our faith than he is in our understanding. He wants us to know him far more than he wants us to explain him. He loves our intellectual curiosity, but some things are deeper than our minds can grasp. But we can experience who he is.

That's why Jesus came. He is the visible representation of the true nature of God. Even the inspired words of ancient Scripture had not captured God this well. But Jesus did. A child who rules, a prince who is really a king, a counselor rather than a dictator, an everlasting Father in the form of a Son. If you want to know what God looks like, this is it. The Christmas story is an unveiling of deity so we can experience God in the flesh.

Prayer

Lord, I want to know you. In this Advent season, give me insight into your nature. Let me see Jesus in new ways. Show me the Father in the child. Amen.

REFLECTION

What does it mean to know and experience God? If Jesus is the exact image of God, what can we say about God's nature?

Further reading: Hebrews 1:3

Lo, within a manger lies
He who built the starry skies.

"SEE AMID THE WINTER'S SNOW," EDWARD CASWALL

4

Prince of Peace

ISAIAH 9:1-7

For a child is born to us, a son is given to us.

The government will rest on his shoulders. And

he will be called: Wonderful Counselor, Mighty

God, Everlasting Father, Prince of Peace.

ISAIAH 9:6

THE HUMAN HEART longs for fulfillment. We want to be satisfied, content, and whole. We want that rare and precious sense that all is right in our world—that our mistakes are redeemable, that our broken relationships can be restored, and that our longings can and will be met. We want the richness and fullness of God's Kingdom. In other words, we want what the Bible calls *shalom*.

That's the Hebrew word we often translate as *peace*, and it does mean that. But it's so much more. It's a state of spiritual, emotional, and physical well-being that resembles the abundant life Jesus promised. It has been used as a Hebrew greeting, a blessing of peace for those who know all too well the fallenness of this world and who long for more. It's an echo of our original design and a hint of what's to come when God makes everything right. *Shalom* is the climate of his Kingdom.

Everyone strives for *shalom*, but most are looking for it in the wrong places—the right job, the perfect soul mate, enough money to buy the things money really can't buy, an impressive reputation, the accomplishments that will confirm our worth to others and ourselves, or even the end of a long to-do list. Most of those desires come from a true need but manifest themselves in distorted ways. They often promise *shalom* but deliver discontentment. They aren't enough.

God knows those deep needs, and he wants to meet them. That's why the promised child healed and delivered and restored lives. He taught truth and offered eternity.

He continues to counsel and comfort and guide us into the abundance of his Kingdom. Because the climate of the Father's Kingdom is *shalom*, the Son is the Prince of *Shalom*. It's why he came.

The promise of Advent is more than a promise of peace. It's even more than a promise of eternal life. It's a gift of the fullness of the Kingdom for all who will receive it now. All of our longings are ultimately met in the Prince of *Shalom*, who wants to fill our hearts with the riches of his presence and restore us with his love. The child in Bethlehem was more than a good teacher and a sacrifice for sin. He is the answer to our gaping needs and the fulfillment of our deepest longings.

Prayer

Lord, grant that I might know your peace, step into the climate of your Kingdom, and offer your restoration to the lives around me. May I live in the fullness of your Kingdom now and forever. Amen.

REFLECTION

In what ways does the Prince of Peace bring *shalom* into your life? How can you cultivate the climate of his Kingdom in the world around you?

Further reading: John 10:10

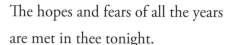

The hopes and fears of all the years
are met in thee tonight.

"O LITTLE TOWN OF BETHLEHEM," PHILLIPS BROOKS

5

Longing Fulfilled

ROMANS 8:18-23

All creation is waiting eagerly for that future day when
God will reveal who his children really are. . . . We know
that all creation has been groaning as in the pains of
childbirth right up to the present time.

ROMANS 8:19, 22

THE HUMAN HEART is restless. Most of us don't need
Scripture to tell us that; we have our own experiences
as evidence. But it helps to have the confirmation that our
restlessness is universal. Creation has been groaning, longing, waiting for . . . something. Anything. Whatever might
resemble the fulfillment our souls crave. Something that fits
the need for eternal significance that echoes in our hearts.

A bridge beyond the borders that confine us to the finite, material world. A sign that life has meaning.

Paul writes about this longing in Romans with a startling claim that what the world is really searching for is a revelation of God's children. Creation is not looking for good theology and convincing arguments. It isn't even looking for claims of miracles. It wants to see God show up in the people who truly know him. And this longing, according to Paul, has been increasing throughout history, intensifying like the pains of childbirth. In other words, the universe has been pregnant with a coming revelation of deity.

Beautifully, poetically, miraculously, the firstfruits of this revelation came through the actual labor pains of a woman finding refuge among beasts of burden in Bethlehem. The restless groaning of creation has since been satisfied for those who recognize God's birth and enter into his life. But recognizing him has been an issue for many. Who would have thought to look in Bethlehem? Who would have expected shepherds to hear the first heralds? Who among today's elites would think to find him in an out-of-the-way country church, or in the streets of the inner city, or in the normalcy of nature's seasons and our mundane daily events? Yet the longings of the human heart are met in places like these for those who have eyes to see him there.

Advent is not just a beautiful story, and it's more than good theology about a divine plan for redemption. It's a rescue mission launched by the God of the universe to satisfy broken hearts and meet our deepest needs. Any human groan is essentially a cry for something that has already been offered in the Incarnation. It may take a lifetime to explore just how those cries are met, but they are. The pains of childbirth brought an altogether different life into this world, and the world has found what it is longing for.

Prayer

Lord, it is not right for me to have Christ yet still feel deep, unmet needs. Show me how my longings are met in him. Satisfy the desires of my heart. Reach into my depths and make me increasingly whole. Amen.

REFLECTION

What evidence do you see of the world groaning for its redemption? What are the deepest longings you think most people have? How are they met in Christ?

Further reading: 2 Corinthians 4:16-18

—⊛⊚—

Long lay the world in sin and error pining,
till he appeared and the soul felt its worth.
"O HOLY NIGHT" ("CANTIQUE DE NOËL"),
PLACIDE CAPPEAU

6

A Long Wait

GALATIANS 4:4-7

When the right time came, God sent

his Son, born of a woman.

GALATIANS 4:4

G OD WAS IN NO HURRY. All of heaven must have
anticipated the Incarnation and the remarkable
unfolding of the redemption plan, but God would not
rush it. For centuries, millennia, long eras of frustration
and futility, the world carried on in the pain of its brokenness, assuming the disorder was normal but longing for
something more. Paul wrote that all creation groaned in
increasing intensity, as if it were in the pains of childbirth,

for a revelation of who God really is. But few people would have identified those pains for what they were. The human heart grows accustomed to the dull ache of a long wait.

In retrospect, God is a master of timing. In the moment, he seems to take an excruciatingly long time to work out his plan or to fulfill a promise. We wait and wait, and assure ourselves he is never late, though sometimes he is, at least by the measure of our time lines. But looking back after the fact, his timing usually makes sense. He knows how to build up to a moment and deliver when conditions are ripe. He is a masterful orchestrator of the divine plan.

So God sent Jesus when the right time came—or as some translations say, in "the fullness of time," capturing the image of a pregnant anticipation—after centuries of prophetic hints and in the midst of one nation's political and religious angst. Some people doubted a deliverer would ever come; others searched the Scriptures and speculated about God's plans for his people. But even in a season of expectation, hardly anyone recognized him as "the one" until he surprised them with his wisdom, power, and love.

The crossroads of Jewish, Greek, and Roman cultures made the timing of Jesus' birth just right. In any other era, his ministry and the subsequent Christian movement would not have had the same influence. But God, in his impeccable wisdom, establishes seasons—not only in an ancient empire, but in your life too. Why hasn't he done what you asked? Why does he seem to be slow about his promises? Why haven't his plans for you unfolded as you hoped? Because the timing is not yet right. When it is—in the fullness of the moment—he will move. And it will be very much worth the wait.

Prayer

Lord, I marvel at your timing and trust you to govern the seasons of my life. Your saving work—in Jesus' birth and in my ongoing relationship with you—is orchestrated for my good. Open my eyes to it daily, and grant me patience. Amen.

REFLECTION

What happens in your relationship with God when you are waiting on his plans to unfold? Do you draw closer or pull away? How might those times help you grow?

Further reading: Hebrews 10:35-38

For lo! the days are hastening on
by prophets seen of old,
when with the ever-circling years
shall come the time foretold.

"IT CAME UPON THE MIDNIGHT CLEAR," EDMUND SEARS

7

Where Heaven and Earth Met

LUKE 1:26-38

The angel replied, "The Holy Spirit will come upon you, and the power of the Most High will overshadow you. So the baby to be born will be holy, and he will be called the Son of God."

LUKE 1:35

MARY DIDN'T KNOW IT, but deep inside her teenage body God had created a remarkably sacred space. All of God's creation is remarkably sacred, of course, but this was an exceptional phenomenon—"the pregnancy of salvation," a medieval hymn calls it. A young girl carrying the Son of God in her womb. The Savior of humanity in her care. The eternal plan enclosed in flesh. The angel's announcement was a stunning turn of events.

Another medieval hymn honoring Mary as a virtuous rose marveled at the merging of heaven and earth within her womb. This baby would be fully human, able to hunger, thirst, cry, sweat, bleed, and die. He would also be fully divine, perfectly in sync with the Father and invincible even in death. We can hardly grasp this convergence—our minds gravitate toward one or the other—but in this case, deity and humanity really did become one. The infinite, majestic God clothed himself in the vulnerability of an embryo in a teenage mother.

It had to be this way. Humanity's stock was thoroughly infected and unable to recover the image of God we were created with. There had to be a regenesis—in us, but from beyond us. The incarnation of Jesus in the womb of a human being was just the beginning of the new creation. The intersection of human and divine would last more than a moment and even more than a lifetime. This was the seed of something big.

The biblical story tells us that we were originally created

in God's image. Obviously, we haven't lived up to that image perfectly; it was shattered when we fell, and though we retain its essence, it comes out distorted in all of us. The Incarnation is a stunning reversal of that trend. The exact image of God was born through a fallen human being. The regenesis has begun. Restoration is possible. We now have the power, through his Spirit, to grow back into the original image. Heaven and earth not only met miraculously long ago in Mary and in the Son she bore, they can now meet miraculously in us.

Prayer

Father, may I grow fully into the image of Christ, who is the exact image of you. Help me walk in newness of life. May heaven and earth converge in my spirit always. Amen.

REFLECTION

How do you think Mary felt carrying God's Son within her? How does the life within her parallel the new, divine life God has put within those who believe?

Further reading: Romans 8:29-30

For in this rose conteinèd was
heaven and earth in litel space.

"THERE IS NO ROSE," MEDIEVAL ENGLISH CAROL

8

The Beautiful Scandal

LUKE 1:26-38

Mary responded, "I am the Lord's servant. May everything you

have said about me come true." And then the angel left her.

LUKE 1:38

THE NATIVITY STORY is one of the most beautiful in all of religious literature. It's the record of how God incarnated his Son into this world to save us. We're inspired by Mary's faith and devotion and impressed with the hardship she went through for the privilege of being Jesus' mother. Her willing response resonates with our hearts.

Sometimes lost on us is the stunning way in which God took on human flesh. It's fascinating that months before he came to us in the clothes of humility and simplicity, he came to us in the clothes of apparent immorality. He knew that a young woman claiming to be pregnant by the Holy Spirit would be greeted with skepticism and derision. A virgin birth is about as unbelievable as a resurrection. Human minds can't accept such absurdities unless there's overwhelmingly convincing proof. And there would be a long thirty years between the mysterious birth and any impressive, public evidence that this child was more than simply human. Mary bore the stigma of having an illegitimate son for a long time—at least among some who knew her story.

Mary's simple faith in the angel Gabriel's announcement—"May everything you have said about me come true"—came before she could even begin to understand the plan, before she thought of the reaction people might have, before any signs of confirmation were shown, before the impossible details could even settle into her mind, and before she could figure out how to maintain a good reputation. The absurdity, the appearance of immorality, the scandal and disgrace, the stones that might be thrown at her, the husband who might reject her, the stigma she might have to live with the rest of her life, the isolation from the community of faith—none of these really mattered. When God speaks, everything else is a minor detail.

That's the attitude we need to have if we want God to do miraculous things in our lives. Our miracles won't come in clean packages. They may be really messy, even scandalous. They might stretch people's faith and imagination to the point of resistance. But when God speaks, the reactions of others are irrelevant. Though his words may seem absurd, that is no indication that they aren't his. When he speaks, the only reasonable response is faith.

Prayer

Lord, grant me such a willing heart that I say yes to you before a reason to say no even occurs to me. May my life always align with your words. Whatever you say, count me in. Amen.

REFLECTION

Do you think Mary was aware of the scandalous nature of Gabriel's announcement at first? How does the stigma she bore foreshadow the rejection of many believers in Jesus?

Further reading: Matthew 1:18-21

Then spake the mother of pity,
"Lo, the Lord's handmaid I am.
Aft the word be done to me,"
and at that point God became man.
"MISSUS EST ANGELUS GABRIEL,"
MEDIEVAL ENGLISH CAROL

9

A Good Man

MATTHEW 1:18-21

Joseph, her fiancé, was a good man and did not want to disgrace
her publicly, so he decided to break the engagement quietly.

MATTHEW 1:19

JOSEPH WAS A GOOD MAN. He played a smaller role in the
Nativity story than Mary did, but his behind-the-scenes
devotion is noted briefly in Scripture and surely forever in
heaven. He and his bride-to-be were given history's most
sacred charge—parenting a child who would also be called
Mighty God and Everlasting Father. If that isn't a pressure situation, nothing is. And Joseph was the man God chose to do it.

Of course, Joseph didn't realize that at first. He only
knew that Mary was pregnant, and everyone knows how

that sort of thing happens. He could have made a scene. He could have humiliated her in a public divorce, which is what breaking the betrothal contract would have amounted to. He could have played the victim. But with integrity and grace—echoing the promise given to David and his descendants (1 Kings 9:4-5)—he decided to be discreet. Only when an angel appeared to him in a dream did he know the real plan, which certainly interrupted his own expectations for how he would live. His compliance was every bit the courageous obedience Mary's was. He was informed of God's purposes and went with the flow.

But the plan didn't exactly flow. Jesus was born into the middle of a heated cosmic battle. Joseph and Mary had to lie low, flee the country, and keep the sacred child safe. They had help—the zeal of the Lord would see to this plan being carried out—but they still had to do their part. So the young parents of humble status went into exile to escape a raging king while the child was still a toddler. They would have to get used to being the center of controversy.

After the birth story, Joseph fades quickly from the pages of Scripture, but he illustrates a profound point.

Many of God's most dramatic works are done on a stage set up by otherwise unnoticed background characters. Jesus is the center of the story, and Mary played a prominent role, but Joseph, only momentarily visible, was nevertheless essential. The massive doors of history often swing on small hinges like integrity and grace. In Joseph's life and ours, faithfulness is far more important than prominence. Nothing is mundane in the Kingdom of God—not even a life of obedience and doing the right thing.

Prayer

Lord, I realize my character is just as important as my big decisions in accomplishing your purposes. May I live with the sacred awareness that goodness, kindness, integrity, and grace are vital building blocks of your Kingdom. Amen.

REFLECTION

Do you find yourself more often seeking to live with consistent character or to make a significant impact? How do the two go hand in hand?

Further reading: 1 Kings 9:4-5

---·☉☉·---

Fear not, just Joseph, this thy wife

is still a spotless maid;

and no consent to sin, quoth he,

against her can be laid.

"WHEN RIGHTEOUS JOSEPH WEDDED WAS,"

MEDIEVAL ENGLISH CAROL

10

The Unfolding Story

MATTHEW 1:22-23

All of this occurred to fulfill the Lord's

message through his prophet.

MATTHEW 1:22

THERE HAD BEEN PROPHETIC HINTS of the coming Messiah—so many of them, in fact, that sages
and rabbis had compiled a pretty good description of
who he would be. There was quite a bit of debate about
this profile—don't sages and rabbis always debate such
things?—but they knew that he would come from Bethlehem, apparently in the time of the Romans. They knew he
would look something like a victorious son of David but
also, from Isaiah's "suffering Servant" passages, something

like the Old Testament Joseph (though some thought there might possibly be two Messiahs, since the latter image was hard to reconcile). They knew, too, that he would be a deliverer of Israel. Still, that leaves a lot of room for interpretation and a lot of guessing as to who the real deliverer might be. The prophetic hints had stirred up anticipation but had not resolved any questions.

That's almost always how prophecy works. It stokes hope but leaves plenty of room for faith. Those who work out precise time lines with unbendable details miss the point: Prophetic words aren't given so we can figure God out; they are given to help us recognize what God is doing when he does it or as we look back on it. Often prophecy has more than one fulfillment—an immediate and an ultimate, and perhaps a few in between. It is divine foreshadowing by a master Author.

Such was the case with Isaiah's prophecy about the young woman who would conceive (Isaiah 7:14). It was given to King Ahaz as a sign about an imminent invasion, but it pointed to much more. A young woman conceiving is not remarkable; a virgin conceiving a child who would be called "God with us" certainly is. When the Gospel of Matthew emphasizes the fulfillment of Hebrew Scriptures again and again, it is recognizing the unfolding of the larger story. The prophetic hints were coming to pass.

Are such prophecies artificially superimposed on the Jesus story retrospectively, as some suggest? Or are they the foreshadowing of multiple seers who got a glimpse of the divine plan over the centuries? The details and fulfillments are too masterful, too laden with still-unfolding significance, too well orchestrated across time to be humanly devised. In Jesus, God was bringing the story line of the ages together. History has meaning, after all. The plot is being resolved. And we find our ultimate purpose by stepping into this story by faith.

Prayer

Lord, open my eyes to the deep mysteries of your unfolding plan across the ages. Let my heart and mind enter into the artistry and majesty of your work. Let me see the hints of your purposes coming to pass—in Jesus and in me. Amen.

REFLECTION

How do the prophecies of the coming Messiah—estimated to be in the hundreds, with some quite specific—authenticate the divine nature of the redemption story?

Further reading: Luke 24:25-27

Isaiah 'twas foretold it,
the Rose I have in mind;
with Mary we behold it,
the Virgin Mother kind.

"LO, HOW A ROSE E'ER BLOOMING," GERMAN CAROL

11

More than Just a Name

MATTHEW 1:22-23

Look! The virgin will conceive a child!

She will give birth to a son,

and they will call him Immanuel,

which means "God is with us."

MATTHEW 1:23

MATTHEW QUOTES Isaiah's prophecy, which was made all the more mysterious by the child's designated role: Immanuel, "God is with us." Even as people of faith, we might be tempted to interpret that promise as a historical phenomenon, as if God was with us in Jesus for a brief moment in time, but now he's gone. No, this is an eternal promise and a very loaded name.

God with us. This is the same God who brought forth an entire physical realm with nothing more than the sound of his voice. The same God whose Spirit hovered over the dark and deep before Creation's dawn. The God who won battles, parted seas, and provided miraculously in times of need. The God who vowed irrevocably to be with his people and never forsake them. *That's* the God who incarnated himself in human flesh as a child called Immanuel.

God *with* us. Not *against* us. Not monitoring our lives to see how far we step out of line and how harshly he will have to discipline us this time. Not watching us from a distance, longing to help if only his hands weren't tied by his own physical laws. And certainly not away on a journey like a watchmaker who set things in motion and left the scene. No, in Jesus, God promised to be *with* us, and Jesus made it permanent when he sent his Spirit and embedded a promise of presence into the great commission (Matthew 28:16-20).

God with *us*. Not just with *them* way back then. Not a phenomenon reserved for ancient Israel, nor confined to a day when miracles happened (or were merely imagined) more often, nor limited to a culturally obscure God of another era. Not the God we can easily imagine loving other people because they are lovable while assuming he must put up with us because he has to. Not a Father who loves because it's in his job description. No, the God who is with *us* is jealous for all of his people and adores those who delight in him. He loves us because we're the joy of his heart.

God . . . with . . . us. The same feet that walked the roads of Galilee are walking with us right now, today. He is present and available. In Jesus, the Eternal One inhabits every moment of our lives. And he always will.

Prayer

Spirit, you promised not only to be with us but to be in us. I want to experience that reality daily—your wisdom, power, and love flowing for me, in me, and through me. May I walk always in the awareness of your overwhelming presence. Amen.

REFLECTION

How does the promise of Immanuel help when God seems distant? In what tangible ways can we sense his presence?

Further reading: Romans 8:31-39

O come, O come, Emmanuel,

and ransom captive Israel.

"O COME, O COME, EMMANUEL," LATIN HYMN

12

Blessing and Favor

LUKE 1:39-45

God has blessed you above all women,

and your child is blessed.

LUKE 1:42

GABRIEL HAD TOLD MARY she was highly favored, and Elizabeth echoed the thought in her greeting. This young relative of hers was blessed above all women, endowed with the honor of carrying the chosen child, the son of the Most High, within her. It was an extraordinary position in history, the culmination of long-ago prophecies and the messianic expectations of her people. Prophecy was unfolding before Elizabeth's eyes, and she could not help but marvel. The baby in her own womb jumped for joy at the sound of Mary's voice. This was an unusual blessing indeed.

But both Elizabeth and Mary were familiar enough with God's ways and his Word to know that "blessed" often comes with a cost. Mary could rightly beam with the honor bestowed on her, but raising this child and watching his controversial and sacrificial ministry unfold would not be easy. She was blessed with an eternal gift and privilege—and also with the turmoil that comes when God's purposes interrupt humanity's agendas. If she had been anchored in the pleasures and plans of this world, she might well have wondered if her calling was a blessing at all. Anchored in eternity, however, she knew God's blessings transcend the sacrifices of the moment.

It has always been that way. The most blessed people in Scripture have been those who endured all sorts of opposition, hardships, delays, and questions. The nation of Israel itself was so blessed by God that it became the world's foremost example in receiving God's wisdom and miracles while experiencing adversity and discipline. Moses was blessed as a deliverer and endured decades of resistance from the enemy and his own people. David was blessed with the kingship and endured years of exile and opposition. The prophets were blessed with revelation from God—and were often killed for it. Blessing and ease do not often go hand in hand.

That's a sobering thought for all who seek God's blessings. His calling, rich with eternal significance, is disruptive to temporal agendas. Nothing he does in this rebellious world is uncontested; as we partner with him, we inevitably enter the conflict of two realms. But the glory always outweighs the pain. The blessing is always worth the cost. Elizabeth was not wrong; Mary really was blessed and highly favored forever. Through her child, so are we.

Prayer

Lord, I am not ashamed to seek your blessing. I boldly ask for your favor. I know it isn't always comfortable or easy, but I choose it anyway. Thank you that your blessing, however costly, is always good. Amen.

REFLECTION

How have you experienced the relationship between sacrifice and blessing in your life? Why is it necessary to remember that God's blessings are always worth the cost?

Further reading: 2 Corinthians 4:17-18

The holly bears a bark
as bitter as any gall,
and Mary bore sweet Jesus Christ
for to redeem us all.

"THE HOLLY AND THE IVY," FRENCH-ENGLISH CAROL

Magnified

LUKE 1:46-55

The Mighty One is holy, and he has done great things for me.

LUKE 1:49

MARY'S SONG, the Magnificat, is filled with praise. Like Hannah before her, who also erupted in worship at the birth of a miraculous son (1 Samuel 2:1-10), she begins by marveling at what God has done for her specifically and moves quickly to what he has done for his people as a whole. She says the proud have been scattered, and princes have been brought down. The humble have been raised up, and the hungry have been filled. These are echoes of Hannah, who praised God at Samuel's birth for breaking the bows of the mighty and governing life and death. In both women's eyes, God has won marvelous victories and provided for the needs of his people. He has done great things.

Of course, no bows were broken when Hannah and Mary gave birth, at least not literally. No princes had been cast down, and no one had yet been raised from the grave. But both women were exactly right that God's mercy for one suggested his mercy for all. They realized what God had done for them individually had much bigger implications. They not only magnified him in their praise; they magnified his works, seeing something universal in the particular. They realized their pregnancies were the fulfillment of God's larger plan.

This is a common dynamic in Scripture and in our own lives. God's particular mercy can be universally applied. When he does something wonderful for someone else, it shows us who he is and serves as an invitation for us to ask him to work in our lives in the same ways. Likewise, when he does something for us, it serves as a commission to share his goodness with those around us. God's acts are prophecies of his goodness that apply to one and all.

Step into the revelation of who God is in Christ. Jesus was not an ancient phenomenon; he's a present witness to the mercies and glory of God. He has demonstrated that God is on the side of his people, that he is who he said he is and will do what he has said he will do, and that he has come to save, deliver, provide, heal, and forgive. He is the ultimate sign that God is willing to intervene in the lives of those who call to him.

Prayer

Lord, you have done great things in Jesus. You have invited me into your mercy. You are a fulfiller of all your promises. May I enter into every inch of every blessing provided in Jesus. Amen.

REFLECTION

In what sense was God's promise to Mary a promise to you? How has Jesus opened the door for humanity into all of God's blessings?

Further reading: 1 Samuel 2:1-10

He has opened heaven's door,
and man is blest forevermore.

"GOOD CHRISTIAN MEN, REJOICE," GERMAN CAROL

14

The Humility of God

MATTHEW 2:3-6

And you, O Bethlehem in the land of Judah,

are not least among the ruling cities of Judah.

MATTHEW 2:6

MARY WAS PREGNANT with Jesus for nine months, but the world had long been pregnant with the promises of God. For ages, creation had been groaning for its redemption, the human heart had been longing for fulfillment, prophecies had built up anticipation, and souls—many of them, anyway—were primed for deliverance. How would salvation come? Who would rise up in revolt? What thundering voice, flash from heaven, or quaking earth would signal the coming of the Kingdom? How would God do this amazing work?

Quietly. At least that's how it would look to human eyes. In eternal realms, this stunning rescue mission likely played out as high drama on a cosmic stage. But on earth, it had to be more covert. If it had been too thunderous, people would have bowed down in servitude rather than faith. They would have chosen the winning side because it was winning, not because it was good. Their hearts would not have been sifted. No one would know who really hungered for God and truth and love.

For all those reasons and more, God was much more subtle. He didn't descend from the clouds of heaven to some great city like Rome or Jerusalem, though such drama is prophesied to come. No, he sent his Son into a tiny town known only for its link with King David and an obscure prophecy in Micah 5:2. Those were significant credentials, to be sure; David's long-latent dynasty was the messianic line, and the Micah prophecy made it clear that a ruler was coming. But the questions of how and when and what he would be like remained unclear. God was coming incognito to the eyes of most.

God has no need to impress. He is completely secure and excruciatingly patient. He has the subtlety of an artist and the precision of an engineer. He is content to dress in unassuming clothes until the eyes of faith recognize him.

That's one of the greatest themes of Advent. Who will be drawn to the plainly wrapped gift? Who will see the drama in the mundane? Who will be bold enough to assume that the star might mean something and the shepherds in the field actually matter? The gift of Christmas is opened to such as these. The God of humility seeks hearts that beat with his.

Prayer

Lord, give me eyes of faith to see you wherever you reveal yourself. Humble my heart to beat in sync with yours. Show me what really matters. Amen.

If you lived in the time of Jesus, do you think you would have recognized him as the Messiah? Why or why not?

Further reading: Isaiah 53:1-2

Today has been born the One without a beginning.

"O WHAT GREAT NEWS," ROMANIAN CAROL

15

The Drama of God

MALACHI 3:1-4

The Lord you are seeking will suddenly come to his Temple.

MALACHI 3:1

G OD MADE PROMISES OF GLORY. When the Temple in Jerusalem was first built in the time of Solomon, and when it was rebuilt after the Babylonian captivity, God promised to fill his dwelling place with his manifest presence. Of course, Scripture is clear that God cannot be contained in a building or really in anything finite. So he came not only to the Temple of stone but to the temple of the human heart—and to the temple of creation itself. God spoke this world into being, watched it fall, cultivated it for his intervention, and then entered into it himself. The incarnation of Jesus was a remarkable manifestation of God's presence in human flesh. The Creator stepped onto the very stage he had created.

Scripture often announces God's appearances in his world as occurring "suddenly." And to human eyes, they do. The Messiah came suddenly to Jews who were not expecting him; the announcement came suddenly to shepherds in a field; God often enters our lives suddenly in the midst of a crisis or in response to a prayer; and the return of the Messiah is prophesied to be as sudden as a flash of lightning or the twinkling of an eye. But God has planned his movements from before the foundation of the world. He often spends millennia setting up a "suddenly" in our history or our individual lives. He may be a master of subtlety, but he is also a master of the dramatic moment. He knows how to orchestrate a surprise.

That's why it's important to be ready for God's opportune times—to see the story line he is writing for your life and respond to his timing. Never mistake his subtlety for tentativeness. His quiet preparation inevitably leads to dramatic moments of his presence. Only segments of a small town witnessed Jesus' birth, but it was nevertheless a certain and monumental event. The seemingly subdued movements of God in your life are building toward certain and monumental events too. His presence is always with you, but his appearances come at propitious moments. He has come to win major battles, overcome huge obstacles, provide for deep needs, and turn the course of your life toward glory—*if* you respond to his movements in faith. Watch and be ready for his "suddenlies." They have been a long time in coming.

Prayer

Father, you are the Lord I seek. Come to your temple—your world and my heart—in power. Make me sensitive to your favorable moments. Fill my life with your glory. Amen.

REFLECTION

In what ways did the people who recognized Jesus for who he was have eyes that were ready to see him? How can you prepare to see his work in your life too?

Further reading: Haggai 2:6-9

God with man is now residing,
yonder shines the infant light.
"ANGELS FROM THE REALMS OF GLORY,"
JAMES MONTGOMERY

16

Behind the Scenes

REVELATION 12

He stood in front of the woman as she was about to give
birth, ready to devour her baby as soon as it was born.

REVELATION 12:4

DEEP WITHIN THE VISIONS of Revelation is a scene
involving a woman and her offspring. We see
highly symbolic images in this scene of Israel, Jerusalem,
and Mary, the bringing forth of God's nation, his chosen
one, and all who would come to believe in him. There are
hints of the primeval Fall and an ongoing war between
the dragon and the children of God. We get a behind-the-
scenes glimpse of the cosmic conflict involving what God
is doing on earth and how the forces of evil are trying to

devour his work. In one short chapter, we have the makings of an epic drama on the grandest scale. And Jesus and his people are in the midst of it.

However these word pictures are interpreted—and many are the interpretations—we unquestionably have an insider's view of the spectacle of a spiritual battle, and there are certainly Christmas themes and images in it. In some ways, it's a snapshot of the Nativity story, which itself is a snapshot of salvation history. A woman gives birth to a son as an enemy seeks to devour him, but the child is spared, and he accomplishes a great victory and rules the nations. In this larger-than-life drama, an enormous, earth-threatening danger is overcome.

This theme is echoed in our novels and movies again and again. An unlikely hero overcomes the greatest of enemies by destroying a powerful ring or attacking the massive empire that would allow evil to reign unchecked. There's a reason these stories resonate so powerfully in our hearts. At their core, they are true. They are reflections of the invisible realities behind our visible world. And they always have a satisfying resolution because the real story does too.

Behind the softness of the Christmas story is a hard truth: Evil has thoroughly infected this world and continues to make headlines every day. The hope of Advent is that God is doing something about it and has actually overcome it. The story will continue to play out, but the ending is not in question. Though the battle rages, its outcome has already been decided. The dragon is cast down, and the child has won. And we have every right, even the obligation, to stake our lives on the hope of his promise.

Prayer

Lord, fill my heart with hope. Teach me the language of promise. Let my words reflect the victories you have won. Show me how to live from a position of overcoming. May your Kingdom grow—in my life and in my world. Amen.

REFLECTION

If Jesus has already won the victory, why does evil still wreak havoc in this world? How has God called us to overcome?

Further reading: Isaiah 66:7-11

The wrong shall fail,

the right prevail,

with peace on earth, goodwill to men.

"I HEARD THE BELLS ON CHRISTMAS DAY,"

HENRY WADSWORTH LONGFELLOW

17

Healed, Delivered, Free

REVELATION 12

It has come at last—salvation and power

and the Kingdom of our God,

and the authority of his Christ.

For the accuser of our brothers and sisters

has been thrown down to earth.

REVELATION 12:10

THE HUMAN SPIRIT IS CRUSHED WITH SHAME. Perhaps you don't know that. You may chalk the burden of shame up to a lack of confidence or a chronic sense of falling short. Maybe you compensate for it so well with pride and self-sufficiency that you no longer notice the underlying sickness. But deep down inside, the human spirit is desperately insecure, constantly seeking honor to make up for the shame, and thoroughly unconvinced of its own worth. We crave unconditional acceptance, significance, and love.

And we have that. We were meant to be free—as secure as an extravagantly adored child who has nothing to prove and everything to enjoy. The cosmic battle in Revelation 12, full of both Advent and apocalyptic imagery, has won that victory. It was the last-gasp effort of shame to enslave the human race, and shame lost because Jesus overcame it. The Accuser was cast away from the throne of God, never to condemn again. Only those who don't know about this victory think the battle rages on. But it doesn't have to. The child of heaven won.

The power of shame is now undone; let the healing of the soul's deepest wounds begin. The child of God, born of a woman, entered into human flesh for this reason. We needed only one human being to win this victory over guilt and shame, and we looked in vain for centuries to find that person. But when Jesus lived without sin, he removed the stigma of our entire fallen world. He represented us perfectly, leaving the Accuser with no rough surface for his slanders to grip. Christ lived up to the rightness and truth of God's character. He accomplished all we needed him to accomplish.

Do not waste this freedom. In Christ, it is your birthright. You did not earn it, but neither should you squander it by holding on to guilt and shame. It was given in love as spoils in the cosmic victory. You are completely clean, thanks to the perfect life that entered this world in Bethlehem and grew up to do battle with evil. The deceiver has been cast down. The truth he long obscured is now written in the brightest of lights. You are an adored child of God, completely free.

Prayer

Jesus, thank you for delivering me from guilt and shame, the cancers of the soul. Grant me to walk in absolute freedom, bathed in your love and acceptance, full of your joy. Amen.

REFLECTION

Are there any areas of life in which you feel lingering

shame? In what ways do you feel unworthy? How might those feelings underestimate the gift of Jesus' worthiness on your behalf?

Further reading: Zechariah 3:1-5; Romans 8:1

No more let sins and sorrows grow,
nor thorns infest the ground.
"JOY TO THE WORLD," ISAAC WATTS

18

Light and Life

JOHN 1:1-14

The Word gave life to everything that was created,

and his life brought light to everyone.

JOHN 1:4

THE WORD WAS THERE in the beginning. He was not only with God, he *was* God. So wrote John, well aware of the extravagance of this claim. But who could dispute it? The child of promise fulfilled ancient prophecies as no other person in history had. Isaiah told us that those who live in a dark world would see a great light, and we did. The darkness could not overcome him, and it still can't. When the Word that spoke the world into existence actually stepped into that world in human flesh, all the forces of rebellion and deception began to become undone. The Incarnation inaugurated an entirely new genesis. The ways of the world may look unchanged to many, but the ways of the Kingdom will prevail. There is now a stream of life flowing through this world that cannot be cut off.

That's the picture John gives us to begin his Gospel. It echoes Genesis for a reason; this is a new creation at work, a fundamentally different kind of light and life that has entered into the world. Scripture affirms the radical nature of the Incarnation. The Anointed One is the leaven in the loaf, the seed in the soil, the treasure buried in the field, the light that pierced the darkness, and so much more. He gave life to everything that was created, and he came again to recreate life in everyone who lost it and has the faith to enter into it again. There's a reason magi were guided by a star. Jesus shines brilliantly, even in the darkest of nights.

The implication is profound. Isaiah prophesied that the people in darkness would see a great light and rise and shine with the radiance of God (Isaiah 60:1-3). The life that has come into the world gives light to everyone—not just to enjoy, but to reflect. Like a glow-in-the-dark surface that absorbs the nearest source of light, we are changed when we sit in the presence of the radiant one. We begin to shine with his glory. We absorb his brilliance and reflect it. By drawing near to him, we become like him. We walk in the light just as he is in the light.

Embrace that mission. It's your calling. The light that came into the world is meant to be shared. Christ has foretold your radiance, and a dark world around you needs what you have. Let his light—now *your* light—shine.

Prayer

Lord, spare me from any false humility that dims the light you have given me. Overwhelm me with your radiance. Let me absorb it fully. May I be a pure reflection of the life and light you have given. Amen.

REFLECTION

How does spending time with God transform us into his likeness? In what ways are we meant to shine in this world?

Further reading: 1 John 1:5-7

Son of God, love's pure light
radiant beams from thy holy face
with the dawn of redeeming grace.
"SILENT NIGHT," JOSEPH MOHR

19

The Regenesis

JOHN 1:1-14

To all who believed him and accepted him, he gave

the right to become children of God.

JOHN 1:12

THE MAGI FOLLOWED the light to Bethlehem in search of a new king. What they discovered was a different sort of king—not the ruler of nations (at least not yet), but the source of life itself. Heads of government rule people, armies, territory, and resources; however, they have no authority over life itself. They can command behaviors, not hearts. But the one who offers life and transformation? That's a greater King. That comes from a much, much higher authority. A King of light and life overshadows all other claims.

How do you honor a King from the realm of the spirit? With a spiritual response, of course. He has no visible palace to enter into, no discernible armed forces to lead, no natural resources to exploit or territories to defend. That doesn't mean he is immaterial—he entered into human flesh, after all, and he did receive offerings of gold, frankincense, and myrrh. But those are tokens of a much deeper reality. They are signs of more significant offerings, investments in the higher realm. To enter into the Kingdom of God, a human being must acknowledge Christ's authority and declare loyalty to him. In simpler terms, we call it faith.

We see that response even in the earliest witnesses to the Incarnation—Zechariah and Elizabeth, Mary and Joseph, the shepherds, and the magi, all of whom said yes to what God was doing. They had no developed messianic theology; they could not have known the full implications of Jesus' identity or his mission. But they entered into the story God was writing by recognizing his work and opting in. Their responses did not depend on comprehending the biblical context of salvation by grace through faith, though most surely grew in understanding later. No, in simply believing, they pointed toward the fundamental nature of the Kingdom itself—that we become God's children when we are born of his Spirit by faith. Once we recognize the one who was born in Bethlehem, we experience a birth of our own.

This is the regenesis that restores the image of God in us and makes us reflections of his glory. By acknowledging the light that came into the darkness, we become lights in the darkness ourselves. The glory of Advent becomes the glory of our own rebirth. We take on the nature of the one whose nature transcends this visible realm.

Prayer

Lord, may my faith always be real—from my heart, full of gratitude, fully aware of who you are. Thank you for my rebirth as your child. Amen.

What does it mean to "believe him and accept him"? What does genuine faith look like in the life of a child of God?

Further reading: John 17:22-24

So God imparts to human hearts
the blessings of his heaven.

"O LITTLE TOWN OF BETHLEHEM," PHILLIPS BROOKS

20

The Place of Presence

JOHN 1:1-14

The Word became human and made his home among us.

. . . And we have seen his glory.

JOHN 1:14

"WE HAVE SEEN HIS GLORY." That is the testimony of someone who witnessed Jesus in the flesh and concluded that he had to have been the creative force that laid the foundation of the world. The Word that was there at the beginning, the *logos* that undergirds all of creation, the wisdom that holds the universe together entered into human flesh and made his home among us. Literally, he set up his residence among us, pitched his tent as the place of God's presence, just as the Tabernacle connected God with those in the wilderness long ago. This human being was more than human. He was—and is—deity incarnate, the intersection of heaven and earth.

The Incarnation was a unique event in the sense that there are no more virgin births on the horizon and Jesus was born of God's seed in a way that no one else is. But we miss out on a lot when we see Christ as the great exception rather than the great example. He was the prototype of more to come, a merging of heaven and earth that is replicated every time someone is born of his Spirit by faith. The Spirit comes into the flesh whenever we open ourselves to his work and allow him to fill us. Remarkable? Yes. But so was the sacred life formed in a young Jewish girl, the beginning of a plan for the ages. It was a picture of things to come.

God has promised to fill the earth with his glory. Whatever was lost in humanity's fall is being restored. God designated a Tabernacle as his dwelling place in the wilderness, then a Temple in the time of David and Solomon, and then a rebuilt Temple after captivity—all of which echo the story of Eden as the first place of his special presence in this world. But God's ultimate plan was not to inhabit gardens or buildings at all; it was to inhabit his people as a whole, and you individually—which is why you were made in his image in the first place. Those who believe in him are to be filled with him. The true temple of his presence is made not of building blocks but of living stones. He inhabits redeemed humanity. You are a carrier of his presence, a vessel of glory, today's intersection between heaven and earth.

Prayer

Lord, show me what it means to embody heaven and earth, to live in both spiritual and material realms, to walk here and now in the light of eternity. Renew me, recreate me from within, fill me daily with your divine life. Amen.

REFLECTION

Think of how Mary must have felt with the incarnation of God within her. Can we feel that same sense of sacredness carrying his Spirit within us? Why or why not?

Further reading: Colossians 1:27

O my deare heart, young Jesu sweit [sweet],
prepare thy creddil [cradle] in my spreit [spirit].

"BALULALOW," JAMES, JOHN, AND ROBERT WEDDERBURN

21

Prepare the Way

LUKE 1:67-80

You, my little son,

will be called the prophet of the Most High,

because you will prepare the way for the Lord.

LUKE 1:76

ZECHARIAH THE PRIEST fell into a common trap. Like many others in his time and ours, he made the mistake of admiring God's works in the past but not expecting them in the present. He did not voice Gideon's complaint to the angel who visited him—"Where are all the miracles our ancestors told us about?" (Judges 6:13)— but he might as well have. His question to the angel Gabriel expressed the same doubt: "How can I be sure this will happen?" (Luke 1:18). Suspicion is never a good response when hearing the voice of God, and Gabriel shut Zechariah's mouth for the duration of Elizabeth's pregnancy. For at least nine months, he would speak no more faithless words.

When his son was born and Zechariah's mouth was opened again, he prophesied in faith. His words were filled with expectation. This son, John, who would come to be known as "the baptizer," would prepare the way for the Lord. John would have a unique ministry of clearing a spiritual highway for the entrance of the Messiah. But in a very real sense, so did his father. Zechariah's transition from nominal to genuine faith signified a profound and necessary shift. Nominal faith would not be enough to recognize what God was doing. This was a time for bold declarations of faith. By opening his mouth in prophecy and praise, Zechariah prepared the way for the one who would prepare the way.

It isn't enough to believe that God once did great works. The faith of the patriarchs and prophets enabled them to see miraculous events, but their faith won't enable us to see any miracles today. God looks for faith that lives and breathes right now. It begins when we recognize the miracles of the Incarnation and the Resurrection—Bethlehem and the Cross and everything in between—but God is still building his Kingdom through his people. He is still raising up those who will prepare the way of the Lord—into their circumstances, into their endeavors, into the hearts of the people around them. He is calling believers to actually believe, to live with expectation, to embody heaven's atmosphere in earth's environment, to be sensitive to his movements, to hear his voice, and to step into the story he is writing. Echo Zechariah's words of faith. Live with open eyes. See the Kingdom, and clear the way for the King.

Prayer

Lord, help me live with expectation. Make me sensitive to your voice and responsive to your will. Fill my mouth with words that prepare your way. Amen.

REFLECTION

How can you prepare the way of the Lord in the lives of the people around you?

Further reading: Isaiah 40:1-5

—•⊙⊙•—

Let every heart prepare a throne,

and every voice a song.

"HARK THE GLAD SOUND," PHILIP DODDRIDGE

22

Lost Hope Found

Because Joseph was a descendant of King David, he had

to go to Bethlehem in Judea, David's ancient home.

LUKE 2:4

ONE OF THE GREATEST crises of Jewish history was the interruption of David's dynasty. The sack of Jerusalem by Babylon in 587 BC meant no one was on the throne in Judah; and even though some semblance of kingship was reestablished in exile and after the Captivity, neither Israel nor Judah would ever again have an independent kingdom in antiquity, with the brief exception of a revolt in the second century BC. Genealogies of David's line were kept during this time, to be sure, as God's prophecy to

David many centuries before was clear: "Your house and your kingdom will continue before me for all time, and your throne will be secure forever" (2 Samuel 7:16). Or as a much earlier prophecy had predicted, "The scepter will not depart from Judah, nor the ruler's staff from his descendants, until the coming of the one to whom it belongs, the one whom all nations will honor" (Genesis 49:10). Yet the scepter had departed, and no one honored by all nations had yet arisen. All seemed lost.

Would a descendant of David's ever rule God's people again? Was the scepter, whether literally or figuratively, still out there somewhere waiting for the fulfillment of God's promise? To the eyes of Jewish sages, this was a faith-shaking conundrum. Many could point only to the magnitude of Jewish sins and claim the promise must have been forfeited.

But God's grace is greater than all sins, and as Gabriel assured Mary, "The word of God will never fail" (Luke 1:37). The promise had gone underground, but it had not gone away. Joseph was a descendant of David, and Mary likely was too. The Messiah did not appear out of nowhere; his lineage resurfaced in one couple of humble means. Jesus was the resurrection of age-old hopes.

There may be moments in your life when all seems lost. In those times, it will be critical for you to remember that there is continuity in God's plans, even when they seem to disconnect. His promises may appear to go missing in certain seasons, but they are nevertheless still there. He is weaving his will throughout history—the world's and yours—to fulfill it. Let the message of Advent rekindle your hopes, however faded they may be. All his plans will be accomplished, just as he has said.

Prayer

Lord, may my heart never give up on your promises. Your words are true; your plans are certain; my hope in you is always valid. Rekindle it and help me grow in faith. Amen.

REFLECTION

What things in the story of your life don't make sense?

Where have you lost hope? What does Advent tell us about how God works out his purposes?

Further reading: Numbers 23:19; 2 Corinthians 1:20

See, the gentle Lamb appears,
promised from eternal years.

"SEE AMID THE WINTER'S SNOW," EDWARD CASWALL

23

People of the Land

LUKE 2:8-20

That night there were shepherds staying in the fields nearby, guarding their flocks of sheep. Suddenly, an angel of the Lord appeared among them, and the radiance of the Lord's glory surrounded them.

LUKE 2:8-9

O F COURSE THERE WERE SHEPHERDS in the fields. Shepherds were always in the fields, far removed from power, money, and knowledge. They were the uneducated who had never studied the Torah, the commoners who eked out a living on subsistence farming, the *am ha'aretz*—the "people of the land."

Shepherds were usually dirty and ragged, and though

they performed a vital service—lambs were pretty important as sacrifices, after all—they were awfully low on the social ladder. Gone were the days of nomadic patriarchs and shepherd kings, though the prophetic pictures of God shepherding his people remained. As a poetic image, shepherds made wonderful symbols in Scripture. But as a profession, it was best that they stayed out in the fields and away from the places of real significance.

But shepherds knew their sheep and their sheep knew them. A shepherd's sheep could recognize his unique voice out of all the others in the fields, and they would follow only that voice. The shepherds did not drive their sheep; they led them. And at night, they kept watch to guard them from all harm.

These are the people God chose to hear the first announcement of Christ's birth. Not religious experts, not nobility, not landowners, but representatives of the masses—a significant sign of things to come. God does not show partiality to anyone; he wants all to come to him. But who are the most receptive? Those who know their need. Those whose hearts are already in search of a Savior. Those who might be minding their own business in the fields and hoping for better days to come.

The shepherds hurried to the village to see the Lamb of God. They told everyone how the fields had been lit up, what the angel had said, and how the vast armies of heaven sang praises. They became the first witnesses of the Incarnation and spread the word in the village. They are a resounding testimony that salvation is not a matter of education, wealth, power, status, or even getting cleaned up first. It's a gift of glory and light to those who have been keeping watch in the darkness.

Prayer

Jesus, thank you that you came for real people, wherever and however we are. I'm certainly eligible on those terms. Shepherd me well. I need your leading and the sound of your voice. Amen.

REFLECTION

If you had been a villager in Bethlehem at the time of Christ's birth, how do you think you would have responded to the shepherds' story?

Further reading: John 10:1-18

The earliest moon of wintertime
is not so round and fair
as was the ring of glory
on the helpless infant there.

"HURON CAROL," JEAN DE BRÉBEUF

24

The Anticipation of the Ages

LUKE 2:8-20

Suddenly, the angel was joined by a vast host of others—

the armies of heaven—praising God and saying,

"Glory to God in highest heaven,

and peace on earth to those with whom God is pleased."

LUKE 2:13-14

IT MUST HAVE BEEN SOME CHOIR. The hosts of heaven are vast in number, brilliant in radiance, and—we can assume—resounding in voice. For thousands of years, they had watched the earthly drama unfold. They had seen Creation and the Fall and perhaps wondered why

God did not destroy what he had created. They must have marveled at the ups and downs of human history, the intricate workings of God's purposes, and the staggering patience he demonstrated as the plan played out. They had heard the prophecies—from the promise that the offspring would crush the serpent (Genesis 3:15) to the Incarnation (Isaiah 9:6-7) to the atoning sacrifice (Isaiah 53) to the end of the age and the creation of the new heavens and earth (Isaiah 65:17-25) to everything in between. They could not have known how it all fit together, but they had watched the omniscient one at work. They must have longed for this day—and this chance to burst into a song that humans could hear.

In fact, Scripture tells us that angels really do long to look into the mysteries of God's plans for humanity (1 Peter 1:10-12). They were captivated by the drama, and they still are. Angels surely look into the past and celebrate the Advent, just as they look into the future and celebrate what is to come (Revelation 4–5). They are ministers and messengers who fight for and care for God's people (Hebrews 1:14) and have been key players in this unfolding drama. They have a stake in what happens. And they know there is more to do. But on this night, they simply praised God with full voices and beaming faces. The centerpiece of the drama, the climactic event, had been made visible.

Much of our life of faith is preoccupied with what to do and how to do it. But today and tonight, just rejoice. Enter into the anticipation of the ages for the marvels of God's unfolding plan. Let this story leap off the pages of Scripture and into your heart again. Savor the moment when God became one of us.

Prayer

Oh, my God, how we have longed for redemption, for meaning, for you to make things right. Bless you for the wonders of your works—for the Child of Promise, the Man of Sorrows, and the King of Glory. On this day, I lay down my questions and give you praise. Amen.

REFLECTION

What sense of excitement would you feel, as a heavenly observer, to see a plan set in motion thousands of years earlier finally come to pass?

Further reading: 1 Peter 1:8-12

With the angels let us sing
Alleluia to our King.

"SILENT NIGHT," JOSEPH MOHR

DECEMBER

25

The Eternal Smile

LUKE 2:8-20

Mary kept all these things in her heart and

thought about them often.

LUKE 2:19

I T HAD BEEN A WHIRLWIND of a year—Gabriel's surprise
announcement, the trauma and excitement of Joseph's
response to the news, the three-month visit to Elizabeth's
home to share miracle stories and be filled with encourage-
ment, a journey to Bethlehem to comply with a bureau-
cratic demand, and now this miraculous birth in a rustic
setting. The shepherds were beside themselves, and the
townspeople were astonished. What's a mother of God
Incarnate to do?

Yes, there were details to take care of and a crying mouth to feed. The days after childbirth are a blur in any conditions and certainly so during an inconvenient journey and with extraordinary stories floating around. Interesting and demanding days—years even—lay ahead. Mothers' hearts can't help but be preoccupied, but they also have moments of reflection. They ponder the magnitude of what has happened, the sacredness and the beauty of the life that has been formed within them.

Especially this one. This experience was worth pondering for more than a few moments, even for more than a few lifetimes or centuries or eons. Mary would treasure these moments, mine them for meaning, and dwell on them for years (Luke 2:51). She could have let the whirlwind turn her heart toward every demanding circumstance. Instead, she let herself fully take in this monumental event.

It's easy to get lost in the celebration, isn't it? The Christmas season has turned into the busiest time of the year for most people. The richness and depth of the day has been smothered by demanding circumstances and people.

Right this moment, many around the world are trying to experience the glory of redemption in the midst of a dysfunctional mess. It isn't easy. But it's good. It's a day worth pondering.

Whatever it takes, spend some time contemplating Jesus' birth today. Let the real meaning of the Nativity—that God is on our side—sink in. The Christ event is still laden with mystery and majesty and all sorts of heartwarming promises from his heart. See each gift as a sign of something much greater, an extraordinary gift of love that cost everything to give and will last forever. Envision your Father as the ultimate participant in the Christmas celebration who wants you to know how he really feels about you. See his face in the Christmas story—and on it, an eternal smile.

Prayer

Father, the human heart expects disapproval and demands from you. Instead, you offer us blessings, promises, and your ultimate gift of love. Thank you. Fill my heart with the richness of this day. Amen.

REFLECTION

How do you think God would respond if you asked him to increase your understanding of and love for Christmas each year?

Further reading: Romans 8:31-32

He whose form no man has witnessed
Has today a human face.

"ON A DAY WHEN MEN WERE COUNTED," D. T. NILES

26

For the World

MATTHEW 2:1-11

Where is the newborn king of the Jews? We saw his
star as it rose, and we have come to worship him.

MATTHEW 2:2

WHEN JOSEPH AND MARY took Jesus to the Temple
forty days after his birth as prescribed by the law,
they encountered a devout man who had been led by the
Spirit to come to the Temple at the same time. Simeon
had been given a promise long before that he would see
the Messiah prior to his death. And, of course, God always
fulfills a promise. So Simeon took the infant Messiah in his
arms and blessed God—with ample references to ancient

prophecies. One of those prophecies was that this child would be both a light to reveal God to Gentiles and the glory of his own people, Israel (Luke 2:32).

So in this drama God was writing, it makes perfect poetic sense for Gentile magi to follow a blazing star into Israel's homeland. Years before the message of Jesus actually began to make inroads into other nations, sages from the East were captivated by a symbol of his glory. This light that pierced the darkness foreshadowed the conflict of the realms that would come; Herod's reaction to the news of a newborn king was a conspicuous sign of the enmity between the Kingdom of God and the kingdoms of this world. And the gifts the magi brought—gold, frankincense, and myrrh—pointed not only toward the honor of royalty but also toward the materials of death and burial (John 19:39-40). The magi could not have known it, but their actions were prophesying the ministry, message, and adoration of a Savior for all people.

The universal mission of Jesus should not have been a surprise to Jews of the first century. It had been prophesied in Isaiah, Zechariah, and many other Hebrew Scriptures.

Perhaps those who looked to those prophecies thought they implied a full integration of Gentiles into Jewish law and faith. But law would never remove the curse of sin; only a radical work of grace could do that. Like a star visible across the sky, that grace transcends earthly kingdoms and cultures. God's rescue mission into this world may have begun with a single clan that became a nation, but Israel was only the seed of things to come. The light is meant to shine into every corner of the world.

Worship the child in Bethlehem, but do more than that. Honor his global mission. Let your life point to the light that shines for all nations. Bend the knees of your heart to the universal Savior.

Prayer

Lord, I want my life to align with the direction of history—your rescue mission to all nations, including mine. Open doors for me to demonstrate your heart for the world and to support your divine plan. Amen.

REFLECTION

The Gospels of Matthew and Luke begin with the birth of Jesus, but they end with a commission to go into all the world. In what ways can you align your life with that mission?

Further reading: Luke 2:25-35

The holy star its news ablazing,
sign of hope for nations raising.
"STILL, STILL, STILL," AUSTRIAN CAROL

27

See the Signs

LUKE 2:36-40

She came along just as Simeon was talking with Mary and Joseph,

and she began praising God. She talked about the child to everyone

who had been waiting expectantly for God to rescue Jerusalem.

LUKE 2:38

SIMEON HAD SPOKEN words over Jesus that were both
marvelous and mysterious; they pointed to salvation
and glory but also to opposition and pain. They were confirmation to Joseph and Mary and other eyewitnesses that
God's work through this child would extend much further
than Israel. But as Simeon was speaking eloquently about

the mission of the Messiah, another remarkable voice joined the testimony.

The Gospel of Luke is filled with stories that pair a man and a woman—Gabriel's visit to Zechariah and then to Mary (Luke 1), the shepherd who goes searching for his lost sheep and the woman who searches for her lost coin (Luke 15), and the persistent widow and the unjust judge (Luke 18), for example. These are clear signs that the Messiah's Kingdom would not be a man's world like rabbinic Judaism seemed to be. Here at the dedication of the child at the Temple, Simeon's blessing is followed by the testimony of a prophetess named Anna. Like Simeon, she was waiting for the revelation of the Messiah. Unlike Simeon, she stayed at the Temple day and night. An old woman widowed at a young age, Anna spent her life worshiping, fasting, and praying. She lived for decades with her eyes open to what God was doing.

We talk a lot about remembering that Jesus is the reason for the season, but our vision should really be larger than that. God moves in every age, and our calling is to live expectantly. Our celebration of past events is genuinely worthwhile, but those who really step into his story are not just looking back. They are tuning their hearts to his voice, becoming sensitive to what he is doing in our day, recognizing the ebb and flow of the Spirit's work, and living with eyes ever open.

Learn to live with expectation at all times. Keep watch for signs of the Spirit's movements. God sometimes surprises unsuspecting souls with a calling; more often, he works through those who have set their souls on alert to notice his seasons of opportunity. Simeon and Anna recognized the Messiah because they had cultivated the eyes of their hearts. Cultivate your vision and tune your heart to his voice, and you will recognize him too.

Prayer

Holy Spirit, open my eyes to see and my ears to hear. Make me sensitive to your every move. Help me recognize your invitations to join you in your work—even today. Amen.

REFLECTION

How can we learn to recognize what God is doing? What are the hallmarks of his work?

Further reading: John 5:19; 12:49

Let us with childlike heart and mind
seek now the Son of God to find.
"CHILD JESUS CAME FROM HEAVEN TO EARTH,"
HANS CHRISTIAN ANDERSEN

28

A Costly Testimony

MATTHEW 2:13-18

A cry was heard in Ramah—

weeping and great mourning.

MATTHEW 2:18

S IMEON TOLD MARY a sword would pierce her own soul. He was pointing to the Cross, of course, though Mary's soul was surely pierced every time her son was castigated by religious watchdogs or the politically insecure. But Simeon was also pointing to a dynamic that would begin to play out in the days and months ahead. Sometime in the first year or two of Jesus' life, when

Herod found out that the magi had not become the spies he wanted, he was furious. And the Nativity story took a dark and disturbing turn.

The massacre of the innocents in Bethlehem is hard to understand. Why did the sovereign God who protected Jesus by sending the holy family away not also protect the infants of the town? Why, when Herod wanted to eliminate the competition, did God not simply eliminate Herod—or at least bind him, frustrate him, incapacitate him, or send him on a long, distracting journey? Why didn't God direct the magi away from Jerusalem in the first place? These gifts of gold, frankincense, and myrrh were a wonderful act of worship, but they cost a lot more than the magi would have wanted. Why did children have to die?

Scripture doesn't give us answers, though many have asked similar questions about atrocities throughout the course of history. What we do know is this: The world has been in rebellion against its God, and the spirit of the world will oppose whatever he does to redeem and restore his creation. For all its warmth and assurances, the Christmas story is really a major offensive in a cosmic war. It's the spiritual realm's version of the Normandy invasion, only more monumental. It had to happen, but it would be hotly contested by a despot trying to hold on to power. It would provoke the enemy's rage.

Even so, it was worth it. The testimony of the magi and even the testimony of Herod's fury give us a glimpse of spiritual realities that we need to see. Surely in that other realm, where light is always shining, the children of Bethlehem now know that their lives, given as part of a campaign to break the darkness, speak throughout the ages. Their blood exposes the enemy. The cries of their mothers convince us that it's worth anything to step out of this hideous rebellion and into the Kingdom of light.

Prayer

Lord, may I never become confused about whose side I'm on. This rebellious world, no matter how much it dresses itself up, is full of hatred and pain. Your Kingdom is true and beautiful—and forever mine. Am

What role did the slaughter of the innocents play in the eternal scheme of things?

Further reading: Isaiah 61:1-3

Then woe is me, poor Child, for thee
and ever mourn and say
for thy parting, nor say nor sing,
"By by, lully, lullay."
"COVENTRY CAROL," ENGLISH CAROL

29

Always Increasing

ISAIAH 9:1-7

His government and its peace will never end. He
will rule with fairness and justice from the
throne of his ancestor David for all eternity.

ISAIAH 9:7

N O WONDER HEROD FELT THREATENED. When magi
from the East inquired about the new king, Herod
was so disturbed that he called the leading religious leaders
for their expertise on the coming Messiah. Perhaps Herod,
an Edomite by ancestry but raised as a Jew, expected
another Moses to rise up and overthrow his intended
dynasty. Or maybe, as paranoid as he could be at times, he

feared even the mention of a rival king in the region. Either way, he responded like a power-hungry dictator and sought to eliminate the threat.

What Herod didn't know—and he was hardly unique in his ignorance—was that the Kingdom of the coming Messiah would be no ordinary kingdom. It would be no threat to faithful and responsible rulers. It had been prophesied by Daniel many years earlier to come when a kingdom of iron ruled the earth (Daniel 2:39-45). It would crush all other kingdoms and endure forever, but it would not look like any other political or military kingdom. It would be deeply spiritual, grow almost imperceptibly, and eventually influence all others. The goal of this Kingdom was to transform the world and rescue its people, not dominate territory. If Herod had truly searched the Scriptures, he might have chosen to become an asset to the true Kingdom. Instead, he was one of its earliest opponents.

Isaiah's prophecy, given hundreds of years before Jesus was born, could not fit any other figure in history. In spite of Herod and any other adversaries, the child in the manger would inherit the universe. And the promise is reassuring:

His government will never end. The verse literally says it will never stop increasing. He will rule fairly and justly forever. All things were made by him, through him, and for him. He is now at the right hand of the Father, interceding for us and giving us access to the throne room. It's an extraordinary place of privilege.

Remember that whenever you think God's people are losing ground. We aren't. His Kingdom continues to increase against all expectations. Remember it also when you get discouraged about your circumstances or your prospects. Know that the Messiah came not merely to teach us a spiritual lesson but to rule every inch of his world—and yours. There is no greater promise of security and abundance, now and forever, than this.

Prayer

Jesus, I bow before you as my King and delight in being a citizen of your Kingdom. Remind me always of my security in you. May your government rule forever—even in my heart. Amen.

REFLECTION

Why did Jesus teach us to pray that God's Kingdom would come on earth as it is in heaven? What does that tell us about his plans for our world?

Further reading: Ephesians 1:19-23

Hail the heaven-born Prince of Peace,
hail the Sun of Righteousness!
Light and life to all he brings,
risen with healing in his wings.

"HARK! THE HERALD ANGELS SING," CHARLES WESLEY

DECEMBER

30

The Zeal of God

ISAIAH 9:1-7

The passionate commitment of the LORD of Heaven's

Armies will make this happen!

ISAIAH 9:7

APPARENTLY GOD gets excited about some things. It's hard to imagine him being careless about anything, of course, but he seems particularly enthusiastic about his core objectives. And there is no more central purpose in this world than the Incarnation. God prepared for the advent of the Messiah for millennia beforehand, and he has pointed us back to it for millennia since. It is not just part of his plan; it is the centerpiece. The reign of the Son has begun and will never stop increasing. He is overcoming the human rebellion and overthrowing impostor kingdoms. He promised to invade earth with the *shalom* of heaven. The zeal of the Lord—his passionate commitment—is relentless in accomplishing this. All of it.

We see that in the birth stories of Jesus. The Messiah was born into a world full of danger, but the Father zealously protected him. He was born under a cloud of suspicion, but the Father patiently yet passionately vindicated him. He came to sacrifice himself, but the Father preserved him until the perfect time and orchestrated our perfect salvation. For millennia, history was hurtling toward a particular moment in Bethlehem. Ever since, it has been hurtling toward the reign of the Son. These events have never been in doubt. When God is zealous about something, it's done.

If God is passionate about this plan, we can assume he invites us to be passionate about it too. He urges us to enter into the currents of his Kingdom and flow with them forever. He wants us to be involved in the expansion of his reign. That means our agendas need to blend into his.

There's no point in trying to build our own kingdoms on the side. That can only lead to frustration. The Lord's zeal is focused on one Kingdom only. All others will have to fit into it.

If you've ever felt out of sync with God and his purposes, here's one way to align with him. God invites you and me to delight in him and have our desires fulfilled, but he wants those desires to converge with his. He wants our hearts to beat with his. He searches for those who will partner with him to accomplish the desires of his heart. History inevitably aligns with his purposes. We find our joy and fulfillment in aligning with them too.

Prayer

Father, fill me with your fervor. Synchronize my heartbeat with yours. Align my desires with yours, so that we may both experience the joy of fulfillment. Let me spend my life delighting in what you accomplish. Amen.

REFLECTION

What gets you excited? How much does your zeal overlap with God's? If there's a discrepancy, how do you think God would respond if you prayed to love what he loves?

Further reading: Matthew 6:10

―――⸎――――

If thou wilt foil thy foes with joy,
then flit not from this heavenly boy.

"THIS LITTLE BABE," ROBERT SOUTHWELL

31

Your Light Shining

ISAIAH 60:1-3

Darkness as black as night covers all the nations of the earth,

but the glory of the LORD rises and appears over you.

All nations will come to your light;

mighty kings will come to see your radiance.

ISAIAH 60:2-3

IT HAPPENED JUST AS ISAIAH SAID. A people in great darkness saw a great light. The glory of the Lord really rose upon his people. The light that came into the world was beautiful and poetic, scandalous and contentious, miraculous and meaningful, and full of humility and honor. God incarnate was born into seeming obscurity in Bethlehem, grew up in an out-of-the-way province of Rome, burst onto the stage with messages and miracles of truth and love, and then was raised up for all the world to see. The story of Advent really has become the story of our own rebirth, the new creation, the genesis in which God is making all things right again.

Though for ages all of heaven anticipated the coming of the Messiah and finally rejoiced one night in Bethlehem, the Nativity is clearly not the end of the story. It's just the beginning. In the New Testament era, the world began to see the work of God in the lives of ordinary people—a divine treasure in vessels of clay—and were drawn to him. For many, no debates were settled, and they still aren't. People argue over the authenticity of the spiritual life to this day. But according to prophecy, we have a significant part to play. The light that came into the darkness is not just the light of the Messiah; it's ours. The closer we come to Christ, the more we take on his radiance. We are filled with his presence and his joy. Isaiah didn't say all nations would come to Jesus' light; he said they would come to ours (Isaiah 60:3). When God's people display his character and live in his power, those who have been groaning for redemption recognize the revelation of his nature, and new lives are birthed.

Few people know the hungers of their heart well enough to put their finger on their source, but when they see evidence of God at work—in the hearts of us, his people; in the circumstances of our lives; and in the power and purpose we display—that longing can be satisfied. A hungry soul has been invited to a buffet. A God who wants to be known has revealed his nature and urged a response. And something miraculous and beautiful is born into this world all over again.

Prayer

Lord, make me a demonstration of your nature. Let the groans of creation be satisfied in me and my fellow believers. Birth something beautiful in the lives of your people again and again. Amen.

REFLECTION

How is God's nature revealed in his people? What beliefs, hopes, attitudes, and actions represent who he truly is?

Further reading: Matthew 5:14-16; John 20:21

Let every voice acclaim his name,
the grateful chorus swell.
From paradise to earth he came
that we with him might dwell.
"GESÙ BAMBINO," PIETRO YON

The light
that came into the darkness
is not just the light of the
Messiah; it's ours.
The closer we come to Christ,
the more we take on
his radiance.

ABOUT THE AUTHOR

INSIGHTFUL AND THOUGHT-PROVOKING, Chris Tiegreen has inspired millions of people through his writings, which include popular One Year devotionals like *The One Year Walk with God Devotional*, *The One Year Hearing His Voice Devotional*, and *The One Year Experiencing God's Presence Devotional*. He is also the author of *Unburdened* and more than twenty other books and has been translated into more than thirty languages. His experiences in ministry, media, and higher education bring a unique perspective to his writing. He currently lives in Atlanta with his family.

.